A Note to Parents c

DK READERS is a compelling readin
designed in conjunction with leading ⌐ ⌐⌐, experts,
including Dr. Linda Gambrell, Professor of Education at
Clemson University. Dr.Gambrell has served as President
of the National Reading Conference, College Reading
Association, and has recently been elected to serve as
President of the International Reading Association.

Beautiful illustrations and superb full-color photographs
combine with engaging, easy-to-read stories to offer a fresh
approach to each subject in the series.

Each DK READER is guaranteed to capture a child's
interest, while developing his or her reading skills, general
knowledge, and love of reading.

The five levels of DK READERS are aimed at different
reading abilities, enabling you to choose the books that are
exactly right for your child:

Pre-level 1: Learning to read

Level 1: Beginning to read

Level 2: Beginning to read alone

Level 3: Reading alone

Level 4: Proficient readers

The "normal" age at which a child begins to read can be
anywhere from three to eight years old, so these levels are only
a general guideline.

No matter which level you select, you can be sure that
you are helping your child learn to read, then read to learn!

LONDON, NEW YORK, MUNICH,
MELBOURNE, AND DELHI

Editor Kate Simkins
Designer Cathy Tincknell
Design Manager Lisa Lanzarini
Project Editor Lindsay Kent
Publishing Manager Simon Beecroft
Category Publisher Alex Allan
DTP Designer Hanna Ländin
Production Nick Seston

Reading Consultant
Linda B. Gambrell

First American Edition, 2006
Published in the United States by
DK Publishing, Inc.
375 Hudson Street
New York, New York 10014

06 07 08 09 10 10 9 8 7 6 5 4 3 2 1

Copyright © 2006 Dorling Kindersley Limited

All images © Dorling Kindersley Limited
For more information see: www.dkimages.com

All rights reserved under International and
Pan-American Copyright Conventions. No part of this publication
may be reproduced, stored in a retrieval system, or transmitted in
any form or by any means, electronic, mechanical, photocopying,
recording, or otherwise, without the prior written permission of
the copyright owner.

Published in Great Britain by Dorling Kindersley Limited

DK books are available at special discounts for bulk purchases for
sales promotion, premiums, fund-raising, or educational use.
For details contact: DK Publishing Special Markets,
375 Hudson Street, New York, NY 10014

A Cataloging-in-Publication reccord for this book is available from
the Library of Congress.

ISBN-13: 978-0-75662-009-7 (paperback)
ISBN-10: 0-7566-2009-0 (paperback)
ISBN-13: 978-0-75662-010-3 (hardcover)
ISBN-10: 0-7566-2010-4 (hardcover)

Color reproduction by Media Development and Printing, UK
Printed and bound by L. Rex Printing Co. Ltd, China

Discover more at
www.dk.com

DK READERS

BEGINNING
1
TO READ

Let's Play Tennis

Written by Kate Simkins

DK Publishing, Inc.

My name is Meg.
I was really
excited today
because I had
my first
tennis lesson.

I put on my new tennis shoes and a comfortable skirt and top.

shoes

Then I was ready to play.

I met lots of other children
at the tennis court.
They were learning
how to play tennis too.

We all shook hands with Dan,
who is our coach.

court

We had to warm ourselves up
before we could begin the lesson.

We started by
marching on the spot.

marching

Then we jumped
up and down.

I circled my arms
like a windmill!

Dan showed us how
to stretch.
"Stretching stops
you from hurting
yourself when you
play," he told us.

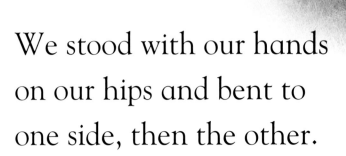

We stood with our hands
on our hips and bent to
one side, then the other.

I could feel my stomach
muscles working.

We tried bouncing a ball
on the ground and then
catching it.

I dropped my ball a few times,
but then I caught it.

Dan threw a ball to Nathan.
He had to jump up high
to catch it!

ball

racket

Dan showed us how
to hold our rackets.

My racket felt light and
easy to hold.
"I can't wait to hit a ball,"
I said excitedly.
"I want it to go a long way!"

First, we tried walking along
a line with a ball on
our tennis rackets.
It was hard to stop
the ball from falling off.

"Pretend you are
walking on a tightrope,"
said Dan.

"Who wants to hit a ball?"
asked Dan.

"I do!" cried Helen.

Dan bounced
some balls and
Helen tried to hit them
with her racket.

She missed
the first few
balls, but then
she hit one.

forehand

Nathan showed us how to hit
a shot called the forehand.

He held his racket in one hand
and hit the ball after it bounced.

Then I tried to hit a forehand.
I was really happy when
I hit the ball.

Samuel is very good at doing the backhand. I watched him hit the ball.

It went a long way.

backhand

Dan said I could try
a backhand after
a few more lessons.
I can't wait!

Helen and I tried hitting the ball over the net before it bounced.

net

We held our rackets up high.
"Watch the ball!" called Dan.

At the end of the lesson,
Dan asked us some questions
about what we had learned.

We got all the answers right and
Dan said we could play
some games as a reward.

Dan pretended to be
a sleeping giant.

We had to creep up on him.
If he woke up and caught us
moving, we had to start again.

He nearly caught me, but
I stopped just in time!

I had so much fun
at my first tennis lesson.
I learned lots and made
some new friends too.

"You did really well!"
smiled Dan as we were
saying goodbye.
"See you next time!"

Picture word list

shoes page 4

racket page 14

court page 7

forehand page 20

marching page 9

backhand page 23

ball page 13

net page 24